D1540329

The Season of Light

The Season of Light

Daily Prayer for the Lighting of the Advent Wreath

Jay Cormier

A Liturgical Press Book

THE LITURGICAL PRESS
Collegeville, Minnesota

Cover design by Ann Blattner.

1   2   3   4   5   6   7   8

Library of Congress Cataloging-in-Publication Data

Cormier, Jay.
    The season of light : daily prayer for the lighting of the Advent wreath / Jay Cormier.
        p.   cm.
    ISBN 0-8146-2468-5
    1. Advent—Prayer-books and devotions—English.   I. Title.
BV40.C62   1997
242'.332—dc21   97-13969
                                                                    CIP

For Sister Romana Walch, O.S.F.

Contents

Introduction

The people who walked in darkness
have seen a great light. . . .

Isaiah 9:1

We are an Advent people—a people who live in the eternal hope and expectation of the ever burning light of the Risen One. The four candles of the Advent Wreath express "our blessed hope, the appearing of the glory of the great God and of our Savior Christ Jesus" (Titus 2:13).

Of German origin, the custom of the Advent Wreath has been adopted by many families, churches and communities. The *candles* in the Advent Wreath remind us that Jesus Christ is the Light of the world. The *circle* of the wreath itself symbolizes the eternity of God and the Father's presence throughout human history. *Evergreen branches,* often used in decorating wreaths, are reminders of the eternal life of God in Christ. Traditionally, the wreath includes three *purple candles,* reminding us of the Baptizer's call to conversion and prayer, and a *rose or pink candle,* symbolizing the Third Sunday of Advent's *Gaudete* call to "Rejoice in the Lord always!"

The Advent Wreath, then, is a symbol of our faith: that light and life will triumph over darkness and death, that our hope in God's providence and love will never leave us disappointed.

A family's Advent Wreath may be as simple or as elaborate as one wishes (four simple candles, of any color, grouped together can serve as the "wreath"). Family members may make their wreath themselves, which might then be displayed in a prominent place in the home. Members of the household may then rotate the roles of presider, lector, and acolyte (the one who lights the candles). To fully appreciate the meaning of the Advent Wreath, the lighting of its candles should take place when all or most of the household can be together, such as before the evening meal.

This book has been prepared as a guide to those who wish to make the wreath a daily occasion of prayer. The structure of the liturgies in this book echoes the structure of Evening Prayer *(Vespers)* from the Liturgy of the Hours: the lighting of the candles (called the *Lucernarium,* from the Latin word for "lamp"), a reading from Scripture, prayers and petitions, the Lord's Prayer, a Collect-prayer and a closing blessing.

The daily liturgies presented here are structured as follows:

1. The *Lucernarium* (the Lighting of the Candle[s])

As the acolyte lights the candle(s), he/she recites the first part of the Antiphon; all respond with the second part.

2. The Word of God

A lector reads the Scripture passage, either from this book or from the family Bible.

The readings selected here reflect the Advent themes of joyful expectation and the restoration of justice and peace in the dawning of the Messiah, Jesus Christ, the Light and Word of God.

The reading is followed by a short pause for silent reflection.

3. Prayers

The presider or leader offers the petitions and all join in the responses.

The Lord's Prayer *is recited together.*

The final Collect and the Blessing *are offered by the presider.*

4. Blessing

The first text is a Scriptural blessing; the second is a table blessing before meals.

The readings and prayers from December 17 through Christmas are found following the reading and prayers for Friday of the Third Week of Advent.

If December 17 is the Third Sunday of Advent, the readings and prayers of the Sunday are used, with the antiphon for December 17 (O Wisdom . . .) *said at the* Lucernarium.

Three candles are lighted until the Sunday before Christmas, when all four candles are lighted. White candles may replace the Advent candles on Christmas Day.

The structure and prayers here are offered as suggestions. Adaptations are encouraged: for example, families may wish to make the intercessions an opportunity for spontaneous prayers offered by participants; groups with musical ability and leadership may want to incorporate hymns from the rich treasury of Advent and Christmas hymnody; those who pray the Liturgy of the Hours regularly might consider including the Advent Wreath lighting with the psalms and prayers of the Hours.

The Blessing of the Advent Wreath

*The blessing may take place on the Saturday evening before
the First Sunday of Advent or as part of the lighting on the
First Sunday of Advent.*

Presider: The Word became flesh
and made his dwelling place among us.

ALL: **And we have seen his glory:**
the glory of an only Son coming from the Father,
filled with enduring love.

Presider: Today we begin to prepare,
through prayer and works of charity,
for the coming of the Lord at Christmas.
This wreath of candles and evergreen
reflects our joy at Christ's coming:

The candles reflect the eternal Light of God,
Jesus Christ.

The evergreen branches signify life and hope.

Our lighting of the candles and prayer each day
remind us that we are an Advent people
who wait and watch in constant and joyful hope
for the coming of our Savior, Jesus Christ.

This wreath, then, is a symbol of our faith:
that light and life will triumph
over darkness and death,
that our hope in God's providence and love
will never leave us disappointed.

And so, let us ask God's blessing upon our wreath,
that the light of the Messiah
will illuminate our home and hearts. . . .

[Pause for silent reflection . . .]

Father of all creation, Lord of light,
all the earth rejoices before your Son
who draws near as a radiant Light
to shine upon those lost in the darkness
of selfishness, prejudice and sin.

Filled with hope at his dawning,
we have prepared this wreath
of candles and evergreen
and ask your blessing upon it.

May our hearts reflect
the light of these candles,
that Christmas will find us joyfully ready
to receive our Savior, Jesus Christ,
your Light to the nations,
your Word made flesh,
who lives and reigns with you for ever and ever.

ALL: Amen.

[The wreath may be sprinkled with holy water.]

First Sunday of Advent

THE *LUCERNARIUM*

As one candle is lighted:

Acolyte: The night is far spent; the day draws near.

**ALL: The light of the Lord has dawned,
shattering the darkness.**

THE WORD OF GOD   *John 1:1-5, 14*

Lector: The beginning of the Gospel of John.

In the beginning was the Word,
and the Word was with God,
and the Word was God.
He was in the beginning with God.
All things came into being through him,
and without him
not one thing came into being.
What has come into being in him was life,
and the life was the light of all people.
The light shines in the darkness,
and the darkness did not overcome it.
And the Word became flesh
and lived among us,
and we have seen his glory,
the glory of a father's only son,
full of grace and truth.

A brief pause follows for silent reflection.

PRAYERS

Presider: As we await the coming of Jesus,
the Light and Word of God,
let us join our hearts in prayer:

That prayer and works of charity and kindness
will be the center of our Christmas celebration,
we pray to the Lord:

ALL: Come, Lord Jesus!

Presider: That all of our Christmas preparations
will proclaim the joy of the Savior,
we pray to the Lord:

ALL: Come, Lord Jesus!

Presider: That this season will be
an everlasting season of peace among all people,
we pray to the Lord:

ALL: Come, Lord Jesus!

Presider: As one family, let us pray in the words
that Jesus, the Word of God, taught us:

ALL: Our Father . . .

Presider: Your Word, O God, has given us life;
Your Word incarnate gives us new life
in the Easter promise.
May your Word illuminate this Advent season,
dispelling the darkness of fear and mistrust;
may your Word dwell among us always,
awakening our hearts to your enduring love.
We ask this in the name of your Son,
Jesus Christ, your Light and Word.

ALL: Amen.

BLESSING

Presider: May the Lord bless us and keep us!
May the Lord's face shine upon us
and be gracious to us!
May the Lord look upon us with kindness
and give us peace!   *[Numbers 6:24-26]*

ALL: Amen.

OR

[Table Blessing:]

Presider: Father, we ask your blessing upon these gifts.
Make us a people of thanksgiving,
that every word and work of ours
may give you praise for your many blessings.

ALL: Amen.

Monday of the First Week of Advent

THE *LUCERNARIUM*

> *As one candle is lighted:*

Acolyte: Through the tender compassion of God
the dawn from on high will break upon us

ALL: **and light the way of peace.**

THE WORD OF GOD *Romans 13:11-14*

Lector: From Paul's letter to the Romans.

It is now the moment for you to wake from sleep.
For salvation is nearer to us now
than when we became believers;
the night is far gone,
the day is near.
Let us then lay aside the works of darkness
and put on the armor of light;
let us live honorably as in the day,
not in reveling and drunkenness,
not in debauchery and licentiousness,
not in quarreling and jealousy.
Instead, put on the Lord Jesus Christ.

A brief pause follows for silent reflection.

PRAYERS

Presider: The first light of Christ appears in the Advent sky.
In joyful hope, then, let us pray:

For the alienated and the forgotten,
we pray to the Lord:
ALL: **Holy Light, come and dispel the darkness!**

Presider: For those in despair and for those who mourn,
we pray to the Lord:
ALL: Holy Light, come and dispel the darkness!

Presider: For those enslaved
by physical, mental or substance abuse:
we pray to the Lord:
ALL: Holy Light, come and dispel the darkness!

Presider: As one family,
let us pray to our Heavenly Father
as Jesus taught us:
ALL: Our Father . . .

Presider: Awaken us, O God, from the sleep of hopelessness;
raise us up from the depths of despair
so that we may be ready to greet
the dawning of the Morningstar,
our Lord Jesus Christ.
ALL: Amen.

BLESSING

Presider: Let us bless the Lord,
the God of the humble and help of the oppressed,
the support of the weak and refuge of the forsaken,
the Savior of those without hope.
To the Lord be eternal glory.   *[Judith 9:11]*
ALL: Amen.

OR

[Table Blessing:]
Presider: Father, Giver of life,
we ask your blessing upon the gifts
we are about to share.
May every moment of life you give us
be returned to you in thankful praise.
ALL: Amen.

Tuesday of the First Week of Advent

THE *LUCERNARIUM*

As one candle is lighted:

Acolyte: The glory of the Lord will be revealed

**ALL: and all humankind will see
the saving power of God.**

THE WORD OF GOD *Matthew 24:42-44*

Lector: From the Gospel of Matthew.

[Jesus said to his disciples:]
"Keep awake,
for you do not know on what day
your Lord is coming.
But understand this:
if the owner of the house had known
in what part of the night the thief was coming,
he would have stayed awake
and would not have let his house be broken into.
Therefore, you must be ready,
for the Son of Man is coming
　　at an unexpected hour."

A brief pause follows for silent reflection.

PRAYERS

Presider: To the Lord of all hopefulness,
to the Lord who gives us every good thing,
let us pray:

That Christ may be the ever-present guest
　　in our home,
we pray to the Lord:
ALL: Come, Lord Jesus!

Presider: That Jesus the Healer may be the hope
of the sick, the recovering and the dying,
we pray to the Lord:
ALL: Come, Lord Jesus!

Presider: That the Risen Christ may gather before his Father
the souls of our deceased relatives and friends,
we pray to the Lord:
ALL: Come, Lord Jesus!

Presider: As we await the coming of Christ's reign,
we join our hearts and voices to pray:
ALL: Our Father . . .

Presider: Hear the prayers of your Advent people, O Lord.
May we be watchful in charity
and awake in selflessness
that we may be ready
for the fulfillment of the Easter promise.
In Jesus' name, we pray.
ALL: Amen.

BLESSING

Presider: Blessed be the God and Father
of our Lord Jesus Christ,
who has filled us
with every blessing of heaven in Christ.

[Ephesians 1:3-4]
ALL: Amen.

OR

[Table Blessing:]
Presider: We thank you, O Lord,
for the gifts we are about to receive.
May our gratitude extend
beyond this moment and table
to every season and every place.
ALL: Amen.

Wednesday of the
First Week of Advent

THE *LUCERNARIUM*

> *As one candle is lighted:*

Acolyte: When peaceful silence lay over all,
and night had run half its course,

**ALL: your all-powerful Word, O Lord,
leapt down from heaven.**

THE WORD OF GOD   *Isaiah 63:16-17; 64:4, 8*

Lector: From the prophet Isaiah.

> You, O Lord, are our father;
> our Redeemer from of old is your name.
> Why, O Lord, do you make us
> stray from your ways
> and harden our heart,
> so that we do not fear you?
> Turn back for the sake of your servants.
> From ages past no one has heard,
> no ear has perceived,
> no eye has seen any God besides you.
> O Lord, you are our Father;
> we are the clay, and you are the potter;
> we are all the work of your hand.

> *A brief pause follows for silent reflection.*

PRAYERS

Presider: Let us join our hearts and voices in prayer
to God, our Father and Redeemer:

That we may seek the ways of God
in every dimension of our lives,

we pray to the Lord:
ALL: Lord, hear our prayer.

Presider: That we may rejoice
in the ever-present love of God
in times of despair, anger, and pain,
we pray to the Lord:
ALL: Lord, hear our prayer.

Presider: That we may recognize every one
as children of God
and our brothers and sisters in Christ,
we pray to the Lord:
ALL: Lord, hear our prayer.

Presider: Jesus taught us to call God "Father";
and so, we have the courage to say:
ALL: Our Father . . .

Presider: You, O Lord, are the potter,
and we are the clay, the work of your hand.
Create us in the ways of your justice and mercy,
form us in your peace,
and craft us in your love.
We ask these things in the name of your Son,
Jesus, the Christ.
ALL: Amen.

BLESSING

Presider: May grace and peace be given to us in abundance
as we come to know God in Jesus, the Christ.
To God be glory for ever and ever. *[2 Peter 3:18]*
ALL: Amen.

OR

[Table Blessing:]
Presider: For your many gifts,
we give you thanks, O Lord.
May our home be a place of warmth and love;

---

may all who come to our table
be welcomed as would Christ.

ALL: Amen.

Thursday of the First Week of Advent

THE *LUCERNARIUM*

As one candle is lighted:

Acolyte: The Lord will give this sign:
A virgin will give birth to a Son:

ALL: **and his name will be "Emmanuel"—
"God is with us."**

THE WORD OF GOD *James 5:7-8*

Lector: From the letter of James.

Be patient, beloved, until the coming of the Lord.
The farmer waits
for the precious crop from the earth,
being patient with it
until it receives the early and the late rains.
You also must be patient.
Strengthen your hearts,
for the coming of the Lord is near.

A brief pause follows for silent reflection.

PRAYERS

Presider: In the name of Christ, our Hope,
let us lift up our prayers to the Father:

That we may live every moment
in joyful expectation of Christ's coming,
we pray to the Lord:
ALL: **Come, Lord Jesus!**

Presider: That we may see the hand of God
in all of nature and science,
we pray to the Lord:
ALL: **Come, Lord Jesus!**

Presider: That we may be always ready to give to others
the gifts of patience and understanding
in unlimited measure,
we pray to the Lord:
ALL: Come, Lord Jesus!

Presider: Let us now pray for the coming of God's reign
as Jesus taught us:
ALL: Our Father . . .

Presider: Gracious God, Giver of everything that is good,
open our hearts to realize your presence
in all of creation
so that we might journey in hope
to the coming of your kingdom,
where Jesus is Lord for ever and ever.
ALL: Amen.

BLESSING

Presider: May the peace of God reign in our hearts.
May God's Word dwell in us always.
In all our words and actions
let us give thanks to our Father
in the name of the Lord Jesus.

[Colossians 3:15, 16, 17]

ALL: Amen.

OR

[Table Blessing:]
Presider: May our joyful sharing
with our brothers and sisters
of every good thing you have given us
be our song of thanks to you,
God of compassion,
Lord of life and Father of all.
ALL: Amen.

Friday of the First Week of Advent

THE *LUCERNARIUM*

As one candle is lighted:

Acolyte: Let the heavens rain down the Just One,

ALL: and the earth will bring forth a Savior.

THE WORD OF GOD   *Isaiah 2:2-3, 4-5*

Lector: From the prophet Isaiah.

> In the days to come
> the mountain of the Lord's house
> shall be established as the highest of mountains,
> and shall be raised above the hills;
> all the nations shall stream to it.
> Many peoples shall come and say,
> "Come, let us go up to the mountain of the Lord,
> to the house of the God of Jacob;
> that he may teach us his ways
> and that we may walk in his paths."
> [The Lord] shall judge between the nations,
> and shall arbitrate for many peoples;
> they shall beat their swords into plowshares,
> and their spears into pruning hooks;
> nation shall not lift up sword against nation,
> neither shall they learn war any more.
> O house of Jacob, come,
> let us walk in the light of the Lord!

A brief pause follows for silent reflection.

PRAYERS

Presider: Let us come before the Lord in prayer:

> For the leaders of nations,
> that "swords may be beaten into plowshares

and spears into pruning hooks,"
we pray to the Lord:
ALL: May your kingdom come, O Lord.

Presider: For the ministers of our Church,
that they may be faithful teachers of the Gospel
and effective prophets of the Messiah,
we pray to the Lord:
ALL: May your kingdom come, O Lord.

Presider: For all who profess the name of Christ,
that they may be heralds
of the justice and peace of God,
we pray to the Lord:
ALL: May your kingdom come, O Lord.

Presider: As one family,
let us offer the prayer that Jesus himself taught us:
ALL: Our Father . . .

Presider: Teach us your ways of justice, O Christ,
and illuminate for us the path of your peace.
Be the light we follow
as we journey to your holy mountain
where you live and reign
with the Father and the Holy Spirit
for ever and ever.
ALL: Amen.

BLESSING

Presider: May God be glorified in all of us through Christ.
To God be glory and honor forever and ever.
[1 Peter 4:11]
ALL: Amen.

OR

[Table Blessing:]
Presider: Father, we eagerly await the coming
of your greatest gift to us, Jesus Christ.

Bless these gifts and bless us,
that we may always live
in the light and peace of Christ,
your Word of light and peace to us.

ALL: Amen.

Saturday of the First Week of Advent

THE *LUCERNARIUM*

>*As one candle is lighted:*

Acolyte: The people who walked in darkness
have seen a great light;

**ALL: on those who lived in the shadow of death,
a light has shone.**

THE WORD OF GOD *Revelation 21:3-4*

Lector: From the book of Revelation.

See, the home of God is among mortals.
He will dwell with them as their God;
they will be his peoples,
and God himself will be with them;
he will wipe every tear from their eyes.
Death will be no more,
mourning and crying and pain will be no more,
for the first things have passed away.

A brief pause follows for silent reflection.

PRAYERS

Presider: Let us now offer our prayers to God
in the name of Christ Jesus,
who is present among us:

That we may rejoice in the presence of God
in every moment of our existence,
we pray to the Lord:
ALL: Come, Lord, and do not delay!

Presider: That we may recognize in everyone
the God who dwells among us,
we pray to the Lord:
ALL: Come, Lord, and do not delay!

Presider: That our deceased relatives and friends
may dwell forever in the house of God,
we pray to the Lord:

ALL: Come, Lord, and do not delay!

Presider: With joyful hope
that the promise of the Resurrection
will be ours,
let us pray the words Jesus gave us:

ALL: Our Father . . .

Presider: Loving Father,
with open hearts and aching spirits
we welcome your Son into our midst.
Make of us a fitting dwelling place for him:
a harbor of peace,
a place of welcome to all,
a community of your enduring love.
We make this prayer to you
in the name of Jesus, your Word made flesh.

ALL: Amen.

BLESSING

Presider: May the peace of God
which is beyond all understanding
keep our hearts and minds
in the knowledge and love of God
and of the Father's Son, our Lord Jesus Christ.

[Philippians 4:7]

ALL: Amen.

OR

[Table Blessing:]

Presider: Bless the gifts of this table, O Lord.
May our Advent preparations for your coming
make us worthy one day to enter your presence
and celebrate forever at your table in heaven.

ALL: Amen.

Saturday of the First Week of Advent

Second Sunday of Advent

THE *LUCERNARIUM*

> *As two candles are lighted:*

Acolyte: In the wilderness,
prepare the way of the Lord!

ALL: **Make straight in the desert
a highway for our God!**

THE WORD OF GOD   *Mark 1:2-4, 7-8*

Lector: From the Gospel of Mark.

As it is written in the prophet Isaiah,
"See, I am sending my messenger ahead of you,
who will prepare your way;
the voice of one crying out in the wilderness:
'Prepare the way of the Lord,
make his paths straight.'"
John the Baptist appeared in the wilderness,
proclaiming a baptism of repentance
for the forgiveness of sins.
"The one who is more powerful than I
is coming after me;
I am not worthy to stoop down
and untie the thong of his sandals.
I have baptized you with water;
but he will baptize you with the Holy Spirit."

A brief pause follows for silent reflection.

PRAYERS

Presider: In prayer, let us make ready for the Lord's coming:

That we may embrace, in our lives,
the Gospel spirit of simplicity and poverty,

we pray to the Lord:
ALL: Christ our Savior, hear our prayer.

Presider: That we may be faithful ministers of reconciliation
and enablers of forgiveness,
we pray to the Lord:
ALL: Christ our Savior, hear our prayer.

Presider: That we may possess the courageous faith
of the prophets and saints who came before us,
we pray to the Lord:
ALL: Christ our Savior, hear our prayer.

Presider: As one family, let us pray to our Father
in the words our Savior gave us:
ALL: Our Father . . .

Presider: O God,
your prophet Isaiah proclaimed your Word of hope
to a people lost in despair;
your herald John proclaimed the dawning
of your great Light.
May we live in the hope of Isaiah,
looking expectantly to your coming;
may we embrace John's spirit
of humility and repentance
so that we may be ready
to welcome you into our midst.
We ask this in the name of your Son, Jesus,
the long-awaited Messiah.
ALL: Amen.

BLESSING

Presider: May the Lord bless us and keep us!
May the Lord's face shine upon us
and be gracious to us!
May the Lord look upon us with kindness
and give us peace!   *[Numbers 6:24-26]*
ALL: Amen.

OR

[Table Blessing:]

Presider: Father, we ask your blessing upon these gifts.
Make us a people of thanksgiving,
that every word and work of ours
may give you praise for your many blessings.

ALL: Amen.

Monday of the
Second Week of Advent

THE *LUCERNARIUM*

As two candles are lighted:

Acolyte: Through the tender compassion of God
the dawn from on high will break upon us

ALL: and light the way of peace.

THE WORD OF GOD

Isaiah 40:3-5

Lector: From the prophet Isaiah.

A voice cries out:
"In the wilderness prepare the way of the Lord,
make straight in the desert a highway for our God.
Every valley shall be lifted up,
and every mountain and hill be made low;
the uneven ground shall become level,
and the rough places a plain.
Then the glory of the Lord shall be revealed,
and all people shall see it together,
for the mouth of the Lord has spoken."

A brief pause follows for silent reflection.

PRAYERS

Presider: With joyful hope,
let us call upon the Lord who comes:

For children,
that they may always possess a sense of wonder
at God's creation,
we pray to the Lord:
ALL: Come, Lord Jesus!

Presider: For the physically and mentally challenged,
that the world may joyfully accept
the many gifts they have to offer,
we pray to the Lord:
ALL: Come, Lord Jesus!

Presider: For the elderly,
that they may know health and hope all their days,
we pray to the Lord:
ALL: Come, Lord Jesus!

Presider: Jesus taught us to call God "Father";
and so we can pray:
ALL: Our Father . . .

Presider: Lord God, hear the prayers of your people
who eagerly await your coming.
Help us to straighten
the crooked roads of our lives
so that we might create a highway for you
to enter our homes and hearts.
We make this prayer
in the name of Jesus, the Messiah.
ALL: Amen.

BLESSING

Presider: Let us bless the Lord,
the God of the humble and help of the oppressed,
the support of the weak and refuge of the forsaken,
the Savior of those without hope.
To the Lord be eternal glory. *[Judith 9:11]*
ALL: Amen.

OR

[Table Blessing:]
Presider: Father, Giver of life,
we ask your blessing upon the gifts
we are about to share.

May every moment of life you give us
be returned to you in thankful praise.

ALL: Amen.

Tuesday of the
Second Week of Advent

THE *LUCERNARIUM*

As two candles are lighted:

Acolyte: The glory of the Lord will be revealed

**ALL: and all humankind will see
the saving power of God.**

THE WORD OF GOD   *Isaiah 40:9, 10-11*

Lector: From the prophet Isaiah.

Get you up to a high mountain,
herald of good tidings;
lift up your voice with strength,
lift it up, do not fear;
say to the cities of Judah,
"Here is your God!
See, the Lord God comes with might,
and his arm rules for him;
his reward is with him,
and his recompense before him.
He will feed his flock like a shepherd;
he will gather the lambs in his arms,
and carry them in his bosom,
and gently lead the mother sheep."

A brief pause follows for silent reflection.

PRAYERS

Presider: Our God is a God of forgiveness and reconciliation.
Let us pray that God's Spirit may dwell among us:

That we may be reunited with those from whom
we are estranged and separated,

---

we pray to the Lord:
ALL: Lord, have mercy.

Presider: That the poor, the needy and the lost
may find honor and welcome in our midst,
we pray to the Lord:
ALL: Lord, have mercy.

Presider: That the sick, the despairing and the recovering
may find health and hope
in the compassion and support we extend to them,
we pray to the Lord:
ALL: Lord, have mercy.

Presider: Seeking reconciliation with God
and with one another,
let us pray in the spirit of Jesus:
ALL: Our Father . . .

Presider: Come, O Lord, free us from our fears,
release us from our cynicism and doubt,
and unshackle us from our own needs and wants
so that we may seek your peace and justice
in all things.
In Jesus' name, we pray.
ALL: Amen.

BLESSING

Presider: Blessed be the God and Father
of our Lord Jesus Christ,
who has filled us
with every blessing of heaven in Christ.

[Ephesians 1:3-4]

ALL: Amen.

OR

[Table Blessing:]
Presider: We thank you, O Lord,
for the gifts we are about to receive.

May our gratitude extend
beyond this moment and table
to every season and every place.

ALL: Amen.

Wednesday of the Second Week of Advent

THE *LUCERNARIUM*

> *As two candles are lighted:*

Acolyte: When peaceful silence lay over all,
and night had run half its course,

ALL: **your all-powerful Word, O Lord,
leapt down from heaven.**

THE WORD OF GOD   *Isaiah 35:1-2, 4, 5-6*

Lector: From the prophet Isaiah.

The wilderness and the dry land shall be glad,
the desert shall rejoice and blossom;
like the crocus it shall blossom abundantly,
and rejoice with joy and singing.
Say to those who are of a fearful heart,
"Be strong, do not fear!
Here is your God.
He will come and save you."
Then the eyes of the blind shall be opened,
and the ears of the deaf unstopped;
then the lame shall leap like a deer,
and the tongue of the speechless sing for joy.

> *A brief pause follows for silent reflection.*

PRAYERS

Presider: Let us offer our prayers to God the Father
in the name of Jesus, the Divine Healer:

That we may give to one another this Christmas
the Messiah's healing gift of reconciliation,

we pray to the Lord:
ALL: Lord, hear our prayer.

Presider: That the Messiah,
who healed the blind and the lame,
will bless the sick, the recovering and the elderly
with health and hope,
we pray to the Lord:
ALL: Lord, hear our prayer.

Presider: That, as the Messiah gives himself in the Eucharist,
we may give to the poor and starving of our world,
we pray to the Lord:
ALL: Lord, hear our prayer.

Presider: In a spirit of reconciliation and peace,
let us offer together the prayer Jesus taught us:
ALL: Our Father . . .

Presider: Gracious God, hear our prayers.
May your Spirit come upon us
to transform our lives and our world
from barrenness to harvest,
from sickness to wholeness,
from division to community,
from death to life.
We ask this in the name of Jesus,
the healing Christ.
ALL: Amen.

BLESSING

Presider: May grace and peace be given to us in abundance
as we come to know God in Jesus, the Christ.
To God be glory for ever and ever. *[2 Peter 3:18]*
ALL: Amen.

OR

[Table Blessing:]
Presider: For your many gifts,

we give you thanks, O Lord.
May our home be a place of warmth and love;
may all who come to our table
be welcomed as would Christ.

ALL: Amen.

Thursday of the
Second Week of Advent

THE *LUCERNARIUM*

As two candles are lighted:

Acolyte: The Lord will give this sign:
A virgin will give birth to a Son:

**ALL: and his name will be "Emmanuel"—
"God is with us."**

THE WORD OF GOD   *Ezekiel 17:22-24*

Lector: From the prophet Ezekiel.

Thus says the Lord God:
I myself will take a sprig
from the lofty top of a cedar;
I will set it out.
I will break off a tender one
from the topmost of its young twigs;
I myself will plant it
on a high and lofty mountain.
On the mountain height of Israel
I will plant it,
in order that it may produce boughs and bear fruit,
and become a noble cedar.
Under it every kind of bird will live;
in the shade of its branches will nest
winged creatures of every kind.
All the trees of the field shall know
that I am the Lord.
I bring low the high tree,
I make high the low tree;
I dry up the green tree
and make the dry tree flourish.
I the Lord have spoken;
I will accomplish it.

A brief pause follows for silent reflection.

PRAYERS

Presider: The Lord has planted the gift of faith in our hearts.
And so, we pray:

That our Christmas tree may remind us
of the shoot of Jesse's tree,
we pray to the Lord:
ALL: Lord, be our peace.

Presider: That we may become living branches
of Christ the Vine,
we pray to the Lord:
ALL: Lord, be our peace.

Presider: That our home may be
a place of love and warmth for all,
we pray to the Lord:
ALL: Lord, be our peace.

Presider: As one family,
let us offer the prayer that Jesus gave us:
ALL: Our Father . . .

Presider: Lord God, may your Word take root in our lives
and may your grace rain down upon us
so that, in our humility and compassion,
we may harvest your peace and justice.
We ask this in the name of Jesus,
the holy Branch of Jesse.
ALL: Amen.

BLESSING

Presider: May the peace of God reign in our hearts.
May God's Word dwell in us always.
In all our words and actions
let us give thanks to our Father

in the name of the Lord Jesus.

[Colossians 3:15, 16, 17]

ALL: Amen.

OR

[Table Blessing:]
Presider: May our joyful sharing
with our brothers and sisters
of every good thing you have given us
be our song of thanks to you,
God of compassion,
Lord of life and Father of all.

ALL: Amen.

Friday of the Second Week of Advent

THE *LUCERNARIUM*

> *As two candles are lighted:*

Acolyte: Let the heavens rain down the Just One,

ALL: and the earth will bring forth a Savior.

THE WORD OF GOD *Isaiah 11:1-2, 3-6, 9*

Lector: From the prophet Isaiah.

A shoot shall come out from the stump of Jesse,
and a branch shall grow out of his roots.
The Spirit of the Lord shall rest on him,
the spirit of wisdom and understanding,
the spirit of counsel and might,
the spirit of knowledge and the fear of the Lord.
He shall not judge by what his eyes see,
or decide by what his ears hear;
but with righteousness he shall judge the poor,
and decide with equity for the meek of the earth;
he shall strike the earth with the rod of his mouth,
and with the breath of his lips
   he shall kill the wicked.
Righteousness shall be the belt around his waist,
and faithfulness the belt around his loins.
The wolf shall live with the lamb,
the leopard shall lie down with the kid,
the calf and the lion and the fatling together,
and a little child shall lead them.
They will not hurt or destroy
on all my holy mountain;
for the earth will be full
of the knowledge of the Lord
as the waters cover the sea.

A brief pause follows for silent reflection.

PRAYERS

Presider: Christ, the shoot of Jesse's tree, has blossomed.
Let us turn to him in prayer:

For the blossoming of the Lord's peace in our
world,
we pray to the Lord:

ALL: Lord Jesus, hear our prayer.

Presider: For the harvesting of the Savior's justice
in our land,
we pray to the Lord:

ALL: Lord Jesus, hear our prayer.

Presider: For the planting of the Savior's wisdom
and compassion in our lives,
we pray to the Lord:

ALL: Lord Jesus, hear our prayer.

Presider: As branches of the same vine,
as brothers and sisters in Christ,
let us offer the prayer he taught us:

ALL: Our Father . . .

Presider: Father, through you and in you,
all things are possible.
May your Spirit of wisdom and peace
take root in us,
so that we may be branches of Christ the Vine,
making your love and mercy
present in impossible situations
and real in broken relationships.
We ask this in the name of Jesus, the Vine,
Jesus, the Root of Jesse's tree.

ALL: Amen.

BLESSING

Presider: May God be glorified in all of us through Christ.
To God be glory and honor forever and ever.

[1 Peter 4:11]

ALL: Amen.

OR

[Table Blessing:]

Presider: Father, we eagerly await the coming
of your greatest gift to us, Jesus Christ.
Bless these gifts and bless us,
that we may always live
in the light and peace of Christ,
your Word of light and peace to us.

ALL: Amen.

Saturday of the
Second Week of Advent

THE *LUCERNARIUM*

As two candles are lighted:

Acolyte: The people who walked in darkness
have seen a great light;

ALL: **on those who lived in the shadow of death,
a light has shone.**

THE WORD OF GOD

Isaiah 43:18-19, 20-21; 44:3-4

Lector: From the prophet Isaiah.

[Thus says the Lord:]
Do not remember the former things,
or consider the things of old.
I am about to do a new thing;
now it springs forth,
do you not perceive it?
I will make a way in the wilderness
and rivers in the desert,
to give drink to my chosen people,
the people whom I formed for myself
so that they might declare my praise.
I will pour my spirit upon your descendants,
and my blessing on your offspring.
They shall spring up like a green tamarisk,
like willows by flowing streams.

A brief pause follows for silent reflection.

PRAYERS

Presider: Let us now offer our prayers
to the God who makes all things new:

For those who mourn and grieve,
that they may find joy and hope
in the Christmas promise,
we pray to the Lord:

ALL: Your kingdom come, O Lord.

Presider: For those who are divided by anger and mistrust,
that they may be reconciled
in the love of the Christ who comes,
we pray to the Lord:

ALL: Your kingdom come, O Lord.

Presider: For those whose lives have been shattered
by physical, mental or substance abuse,
that they may make their lives new again
in the hope of the Messiah,
we pray to the Lord:

ALL: Your kingdom come, O Lord.

Presider: Let us seek the forgiveness of God
and of one another
by offering the prayer Jesus taught us:

ALL: Our Father . . .

Presider: O God, you constantly call us to new beginnings,
to make all things new again and again.
May your Spirit of reconciliation and forgiveness
make us sharers in your work of creation,
that we may remake our world
in your justice, hope and peace.
We ask in the name of your Son,
Jesus Christ, the Prince of Peace.

ALL: Amen.

BLESSING

Presider: May the peace of God
which is beyond all understanding
keep our hearts and minds
in the knowledge and love of God

---

and of the Father's Son, our Lord Jesus Christ.

[Philippians 4:7]

ALL: Amen.

OR

[Table Blessing:]

Presider: Bless the gifts of this table, O Lord.
May our Advent preparations for your coming
make us worthy one day to enter your presence
and celebrate forever at your table in heaven.

ALL: Amen.

Third Sunday of Advent

THE *LUCERNARIUM*

As three candles are lighted:

Acolyte: Rejoice! The Lord is near!

ALL: Rejoice! The Sun of justice and peace dawns!

THE WORD OF GOD   *Philippians 4:4-7*

Lector: From Paul's letter to the Philippians.

Rejoice in the Lord always;
again I will say, Rejoice.
Let your gentleness be known to everyone.
The Lord is near.
Do not worry about anything,
but in everything by prayer
and supplication with thanksgiving
let your requests be made known to God.
And the peace of God,
which surpasses all understanding,
will guard your hearts and minds in Christ Jesus.

A brief pause follows for silent reflection.

PRAYERS

Presider: Our joy is the Lord, who hears our prayers:

That our Christmas preparations
will proclaim the joy of the Savior,
we pray to the Lord:
ALL: Come, Lord, joy of your people!

Presider: That our hospitality to our visitors and guests
may proclaim the love of the Savior,
we pray to the Lord:
ALL: Come, Lord, joy of your people!

Presider: That our compassionate help to those in need
may proclaim the compassion of the Savior,
we pray to the Lord:
ALL: Come, Lord, joy of your people!

Presider: Jesus revealed to us
the immense love of God as our Father;
and so, we joyfully pray:
ALL: Our Father . . .

Presider: Gracious God, you are our hope
who never disappoints us;
you are our joy
who turns our mourning into dancing;
you are our Father
whose love for us is unconditional
and without limit.
With humility and hope,
with the conviction of faith,
with the hope you inspire,
may the Advent journeys of our lives
bring us to the fulfillment
of the Easter promise of Christ Jesus,
in whose name we pray.
ALL: Amen.

BLESSING

Presider: May the Lord bless us and keep us!
May the Lord's face shine upon us
and be gracious to us!
May the Lord look upon us with kindness
and give us peace!   *[Numbers 6:24-26]*
ALL: Amen.

OR

[Table Blessing:]
Presider: Father, we ask your blessing upon these gifts.
Make us a people of thanksgiving,
that every word and work of ours

may give you praise for your many blessings.
ALL: Amen.

Monday of the Third Week of Advent

THE *LUCERNARIUM*

As three candles are lighted:

Acolyte: Through the tender compassion of God
the dawn from on high will break upon us

ALL: and light the way of peace.

THE WORD OF GOD   *Isaiah 49:13, 15-16*

Lector: From the prophet Isaiah.

Sing for joy, O heavens,
and exult, O earth;
break forth, O mountains, into singing!
For the Lord has comforted his people,
and will have compassion on his suffering ones.
Can a woman forget her nursing child,
or show no compassion for the child of her womb?
Even these may forget,
yet I will not forget you.
See, I have inscribed you on the palms of my hands.

A brief pause follows for silent reflection.

PRAYERS

Presider: Let us now raise our hearts and voices in prayer
to the Lord who saves us:

For parents and guardians,
that they may love their children
as God loves every one of us,
we pray to the Lord:
ALL: Loving Father, hear our prayer.

Presider: For children,
especially children who are poor,

abused and forgotten,
that the love of God may be real to them
in the compassion and care of others,
we pray to the Lord:

ALL: Loving Father, hear our prayer.

Presider: For families and households,
that they may always realize the joy
of Jesus' presence in their midst,
we pray to the Lord:

ALL: Loving Father, hear our prayer.

Presider: As children of God
and brothers and sisters in Christ,
let us pray as Jesus taught us:

ALL: Our Father . . .

Presider: Gracious God,
in your wisdom and justice
you are Father to us;
in your compassion and mercy
you are Mother to us.
As you love us,
may we, in turn, love one another
without limit, condition or expectation.
We ask this in the name of your Son,
Jesus, the Christ.

ALL: Amen.

BLESSING

Presider: Let us bless the Lord,
the God of the humble and help of the oppressed,
the support of the weak and refuge of the forsaken,
the Savior of those without hope.
To the Lord be eternal glory.   *[Judith 9:11]*

ALL: Amen.

OR

[Table Blessing:]

Presider: Father, Giver of life,
we ask your blessing upon the gifts
we are about to share.
May every moment of life you give us
be returned to you in thankful praise.

ALL: Amen.

Tuesday of the Third Week of Advent

THE *LUCERNARIUM*

As three candles are lighted:

Acolyte: The glory of the Lord will be revealed

**ALL: and all humankind will see
the saving power of God.**

THE WORD OF GOD   *Ezekiel 34:11-15*

Lector: From the prophet Ezekiel.

Thus says the Lord God:
I myself will search for my sheep,
and I will seek them out.
As shepherds seek out their flocks
when they are among their scattered sheep,
so I will seek out my sheep.
I will rescue them from all the places
to which they have been scattered
on a day of clouds and thick darkness.
I will bring them out from the peoples
and gather them from the countries,
and I will bring them to their own land;
and I will feed them on the mountains of Israel,
by the watercourses,
and in all the inhabited parts of the land.
I will feed them with good pasture;
there they shall lie down in good grazing land,
and they shall feed on rich pasture
on the mountains of Israel.
I myself will be the shepherd of my sheep,
and I will make them all lie down,
says the Lord God.

A brief pause follows for silent reflection.

PRAYERS

Presider: Let us offer our prayers to the Lord,
our loving and compassionate Shepherd:

For the nations and peoples of the world,
that God may gather and shepherd them
in holy peace,
we pray to the Lord:
ALL: Good Shepherd, hear your people's cry.

Presider: For those suffering from illness,
abuse or alienation,
that the Savior will bind up
their broken bodies
and heal their broken spirits,
we pray to the Lord:
ALL: Good Shepherd, hear your people's cry.

Presider: For those who will return to the Lord
this Christmas,
that they may live forever in the presence of God,
we pray to the Lord:
ALL: Good Shepherd, hear your people's cry.

Presider: Christ our Shepherd guides us to God.
Let us join our hearts and voices
to offer the prayer he taught us:
ALL: Our Father . . .

Presider: O Saving God, you have gathered us together
and transformed us into your holy people.
Renew us in spirit and consecrate us in love
that we may journey in peace and joy
to your holy mountain.
We ask this in the name of your Son,
Jesus, the Good Shepherd.
ALL: Amen.

BLESSING

Presider: Blessed be the God and Father
of our Lord Jesus Christ,
who has filled us
with every blessing of heaven in Christ.

[Ephesians 1:3-4]

ALL: Amen.

OR

[Table Blessing:]
Presider: We thank you, O Lord,
for the gifts we are about to receive.
May our gratitude extend
beyond this moment and table
to every season and every place.

ALL: Amen.

Wednesday of the
Third Week of Advent

THE *LUCERNARIUM*

As three candles are lighted:

Acolyte: When peaceful silence lay over all,
and night had run half its course,

**ALL: your all-powerful Word, O Lord,
leapt down from heaven.**

THE WORD OF GOD   *Baruch 4:36; 5:1-5*

Lector: From the prophet Baruch.

Look toward the east, Jerusalem,
and see the joy that is coming to you from God.
Take off the garment of your sorrow and affliction,
O Jerusalem,
and put on forever the beauty of the glory
from God.
Put on the robe of righteousness that comes
from God;
put on your head the diadem
of the glory of the Everlasting;
for God will show your splendor
everywhere under heaven.
For God will give you evermore the name
"Righteous Peace, Godly Glory."
Arise, Jerusalem, stand upon the height;
look toward the east,
and see your children gathered from west and east
at the word of the Holy One,
rejoicing that God has remembered them.

A brief pause follows for silent reflection.

PRAYERS

Presider: The Lord is the Joy of the humble
and the Treasure of the poor.
Let us turn to our God in prayer:

For the troubled and despairing,
that they may find new hope
in our compassion and care,
we pray to the Lord:
ALL: Lord, bless us with your peace.

Presider: For those who are persecuted for their faith,
that their suffering and witness
may one day be exalted before God,
we pray to the Lord:
ALL: Lord, bless us with your peace.

Presider: For the starving and homeless,
that we may see in them the face of Christ,
we pray to the Lord:
ALL: Lord, bless us with your peace.

Presider: Jesus taught us to call God "Father";
and so, we joyfully pray:
ALL: Our Father . . .

Presider: Come, O Holy Redeemer!
Remove our despair and restore us in hope;
dispel our self-centeredness
and reconcile us with you and with one another;
heal our pain and brokenness
and make us whole and complete
in the love of our Redeemer, Jesus Christ,
in whose name we offer our prayer.
ALL: Amen.

BLESSING

Presider: May grace and peace be given to us in abundance
as we come to know God in Jesus, the Christ.

To God be glory for ever and ever.   *[2 Peter 3:18]*

ALL: Amen.

OR

[Table Blessing:]

Presider: For your many gifts,
we give you thanks, O Lord.
May our home be a place of warmth and love;
may all who come to our table
be welcomed as would Christ.

ALL: Amen.

Thursday of the
Third Week of Advent

THE *LUCERNARIUM*

As three candles are lighted:

Acolyte: The Lord will give this sign:
A virgin will give birth to a Son:

**ALL: and his name will be "Emmanuel"—
"God is with us."**

THE WORD OF GOD   *Isaiah 25:6, 7-10*

Lector: From the prophet Isaiah.

On this mountain
the Lord of hosts will make for all peoples
a feast of rich food,
a feast of well-aged wines.
And he will destroy on this mountain
the shroud that is cast over all peoples,
the sheet that is spread over all nations;
he will swallow up death forever.
Then the Lord God will wipe away
the tears from all faces,
and the disgrace of his people
he will take away from all the earth,
for the Lord has spoken.
It will be said on that day,
Lo, this is our God;
we have waited for him,
so that he might save us.
This is the Lord for whom we have waited;
let us be glad and rejoice in his salvation.
For the hand of the Lord will rest on this mountain.

A brief pause follows for silent reflection.

PRAYERS

Presider: The Lord comes to save us;
with joy and in hope, then, we pray:

For our Church and parish,
that the Bread of life may unite us
as a community of the Resurrection,
we pray to the Lord:

ALL: Lord, hear our prayer.

Presider: For churches and faith communities,
that they may find unity in our common journey
to God's holy mountain,
we pray to the Lord:

ALL: Lord, hear our prayer.

Presider: For the nations and peoples of the world,
that Isaiah's vision may be realized in every land,
we pray to the Lord:

ALL: Lord, hear our prayer.

Presider: As one family,
let us offer together the prayer that Jesus gave us:

ALL: Our Father . . .

Presider: Come, O Lord, burn away the clouds of despair
and clear away the mist of sadness that engulfs us.
Arise and illuminate our journey
to your holy mountain
with your peace and justice.
We ask this in the name of Jesus, the Bread of life.

ALL: Amen.

BLESSING

Presider: May the peace of God reign in our hearts.
May God's Word dwell in us always.
In all our words and actions
let us give thanks to our Father
in the name of the Lord Jesus.

ALL: Amen.

OR

[Table Blessing:]
Presider: May our joyful sharing
with our brothers and sisters
of every good thing you have given us
be our song of thanks to you,
God of compassion,
Lord of life and Father of all.
ALL: Amen.

Friday of the Third Week of Advent

THE *LUCERNARIUM*

As three candles are lighted:

Acolyte: Let the heavens rain down the Just One,

ALL: and the earth will bring forth a Savior.

THE WORD OF GOD   *Titus 2:11-13*

Lector: From Paul's letter to Titus.

The grace of God has appeared,
bringing salvation to all,
training us to renounce impiety and worldly
    passions,
and in the present age to live lives
that are self-controlled, upright and godly,
while we wait for the blessed hope
and the manifestation of the glory
of our great God and Savior, Jesus Christ.

A brief pause follows for silent reflection.

PRAYERS

Presider: The Lord is with us!
Let us call upon our God in prayer:

That our home may be a fitting dwelling
for the Lord who comes,
we pray to the Lord:
ALL: Christ Jesus, hear our prayer.

Presider: That, in good times,
we may rejoice in thanksgiving
for God's countless blessings to us,
we pray to the Lord:
ALL: Christ Jesus, hear our prayer.

Presider: That, in times of difficulty and pain,
we may realize God's healing presence among us,
we pray to the Lord:
ALL: Christ Jesus, hear our prayer.

Presider: In Christ, God's love has been made real to us.
In hope, then, we dare to pray:
ALL: Our Father . . .

Presider: Father of all goodness,
with gratitude, we remember Jesus' humanity,
this life he shared with us;
with hope, we celebrate his Resurrection,
the life he promises us.
May our dedication to his Gospel
of peace and reconciliation
make us worthy of the life of the world to come.
We ask this in the name of your Son,
Jesus, your Love incarnate.
ALL: Amen.

BLESSING

Presider: May God be glorified in all of us through Christ.
To God be glory and honor forever and ever.
[1 Peter 4:11]

    ALL: Amen.

    OR

    [Table Blessing:]
Presider: Father, we eagerly await the coming
of your greatest gift to us, Jesus Christ.
Bless these gifts and bless us,
that we may always live
in the light and peace of Christ,
your Word of light and peace to us.
ALL: Amen.

December 17

THE *LUCERNARIUM*

As three or four candles are lighted:

Acolyte: O Wisdom, O holy Word of God,
you govern all creation
with your strong yet tender care:

ALL: Come, show your people the way to salvation!

THE WORD OF GOD   *Hebrews 1:1-3*

Lector: The beginning of the letter to the Hebrews.

Long ago God spoke to our ancestors
in many and various ways by the prophets,
but in these last days
he has spoken to us by a Son,
whom he appointed heir of all things,
through whom he also created the worlds.
He is the reflection of God's glory
and the exact imprint of God's very being,
and he sustains all things by his powerful word.

A brief pause follows for silent reflection.

PRAYERS

Presider: In Christ Jesus,
we have seen and touched the glory of God.
In his name, let us pray:

For our neighbors of other nations and lands,
our brothers and sisters in the Father,
we pray to the Lord:
ALL: O holy Word of God, hear us!

Presider: For our Jewish friends,
our ancestors in the faith,

we pray to the Lord:
ALL: O holy Word of God, hear us!

Presider: For each of us,
Christians called to reflect the Father's glory,
we pray to the Lord:
ALL: O holy Word of God, hear us!

Presider: Let us now join our hearts as one
to pray the words that Jesus gave his friends:
ALL: Our Father . . .

Presider: O God,
in Christ, you speak your Word
of peace, justice and compassion.
Open our spirits to hear your Word,
open our hearts to welcome your Word,
open our hands to bring your Word
into our family and community.
We ask this in the name of your Son,
Jesus, your Word made flesh.
ALL: Amen.

BLESSING

Presider: May the Lord bless us and keep us!
May the Lord's face shine upon us
and be gracious to us!
May the Lord look upon us with kindness
and give us peace!   *[Numbers 6:24-26]*
ALL: Amen.

OR

[Table Blessing:]
Presider: Father, we ask your blessing upon these gifts.
Make us a people of thanksgiving,
that every word and work of ours
may give you praise for your many blessings.
ALL: Amen.

December 18

THE *LUCERNARIUM*

As three or four candles are lighted:

Acolyte: O holy Lord of Israel,
who showed yourself to Moses
in the burning bush,
who gave him the holy law
on the mountain of Sinai:

ALL: Come, stretch out your mighty hand to set us free!

THE WORD OF GOD   *Zephaniah 3:14, 17, 20*

Lector: From the prophet Zephaniah.

Sing aloud, O daughter Zion;
shout, O Israel!
Rejoice and exult with all your heart,
O daughter Jerusalem!
The Lord, your God, is in your midst;
he will renew you in his love.
At that time I will bring you home,
at the time when I gather you;
for I will make you renowned and praised
among all the peoples of the earth,
when I restore your fortunes before your eyes,
says the Lord.

A brief pause follows for silent reflection.

PRAYERS

Presider: To God, who illuminates this season with holy light,
let us pray:

That God will bless those who will be receiving
our Christmas cards and letters in the days ahead,

we pray to the Lord:

ALL: **O Lord of holiness, hear our prayer!**

Presider: That the gifts we exchange this Christmas
will include the gifts of love and understanding,
we pray to the Lord:

ALL: **O Lord of holiness, hear our prayer!**

Presider: That our home may rejoice
in the Lord's presence among us
in every season,
we pray to the Lord:

ALL: **O Lord of holiness, hear our prayer!**

Presider: As one family,
let us pray to our heavenly Father
in the words that Jesus taught us:

ALL: **Our Father . . .**

Presider: O Lord, restore our land with peace,
renew our hearts in love,
lift our spirits in hope,
so that we may joyfully welcome into our midst
your Son, Jesus Christ, our Savior,
in whose name we offer our prayer.

ALL: **Amen.**

BLESSING

Presider: Let us bless the Lord,
the God of the humble and help of the oppressed,
the support of the weak and refuge of the forsaken,
the Savior of those without hope.
To the Lord be eternal glory.   *[Judith 9:11]*

ALL: **Amen.**

OR

[Table Blessing:]
Presider: Father, Giver of life,
we ask your blessing upon the gifts

we are about to share.
May every moment of life you give us
be returned to you in thankful praise.
ALL: Amen.

December 19

THE *LUCERNARIUM*

As three or four candles are lighted:

Acolyte: O Flower of Jesse's stem,
sign of God's love for us:

ALL: Come, save us without delay!

THE WORD OF GOD   *Jeremiah 33:14-16*

Lector: From the prophet Jeremiah.

The days are surely coming, says the Lord,
when I will fulfill the promise I made
to the house of Israel and the house of Judah.
In those days and at that time
I will cause a righteous Branch
to spring up for David;
and he shall execute justice and righteousness
    in the land.
In those days Judah will be saved
and Jerusalem will live in safety.
And this is the name by which it will be called:
"The Lord is our righteousness."

A brief pause follows for silent reflection.

PRAYERS

Presider: In Christ, God's promise to us has been fulfilled.
In confidence, then, let us pray:

That the love of Christ
may be the foundation of our life together,
we pray to the Lord:
ALL: O Flower of Jesse's stem, hear us!

Presider: That the spirit of God's peace may dwell

in all families, communities and nations,
we pray to the Lord:

ALL: O Flower of Jesse's stem, hear us!

Presider: That we may seek the justice and mercy of God
in every relationship, decision and choice we make,
we pray to the Lord:

ALL: O Flower of Jesse's stem, hear us!

Presider: Jesus taught us to call God "Father";
and so, we pray with confidence:

ALL: Our Father . . .

Presider: God of mercy, Lord of compassion,
your holy will is justice for the poor
and peace for the afflicted.
May Christ, your Word,
pierce our hearts and inflame our spirits
to proclaim your reign of justice and peace.
We ask this in the name of your Son,
Jesus, the Messiah.

ALL: Amen.

BLESSING

Presider: Blessed be the God and Father
of our Lord Jesus Christ,
who has filled us
with every blessing of heaven in Christ.

[Ephesians 1:3-4]

ALL: Amen.

OR

[Table Blessing:]
Presider: We thank you, O Lord,
for the gifts we are about to receive.
May our gratitude extend
beyond this moment and table
to every season and every place.

ALL: Amen.

December 20

THE *LUCERNARIUM*

> *As three or four candles are lighted:*

Acolyte: O Key of David,
opening the gates of God's dwelling place:

ALL: **Come, break down the prison walls of death
and lead your captive people into your freedom!**

THE WORD OF GOD *Luke 1:26-38*

Lector: From the Gospel of Luke.

The angel Gabriel was sent by God
to a town in Galilee called Nazareth,
to a virgin engaged to a man whose name was
    Joseph,
of the house of David.
The virgin's name was Mary.
And he came to her and said,
"Greetings, favored one!
The Lord is with you."
But she was much perplexed by his words
and pondered what sort of greeting this might be.
The angel said to her,
"Do not be afraid, Mary,
for you have found favor with God.
And now, you will conceive in your womb
    and bear a son,
and you will name him Jesus.
He will be great,
and will be called the Son of the Most High,
and the Lord God will give to him
the throne of his ancestor David.
He will reign over the house of Jacob forever,
and of his kingdom there will be no end."
Mary said to the angel,

"How can this be, since I am a virgin?"
The angel said to her,
"The Holy Spirit will come upon you,
and the power of the Most High will overshadow
   you;
therefore the child to be born will be holy;
he will be called Son of God.
And now, your relative Elizabeth in her old age
has also conceived a son;
and this is the sixth month
for her who was said to be barren.
For nothing is impossible with God."
Then Mary said,
"Here I am, the servant of the Lord;
let it be with me according to your word."

A brief pause follows for silent reflection.

PRAYERS

Presider: We now make our prayer to the Father
through Jesus, the Savior born of Mary:

That we may be open to the will of God,
as was Mary to Gabriel's news,
we pray to the Lord:
ALL: O Key of David, open for us the way to God!

Presider: That we may joyfully accept the call
to embrace the good news of Christ,
as did Mary, the "first disciple,"
we pray to the Lord:
ALL: O Key of David, open for us the way to God!

Presider: That we may keep faith in times of difficulty,
as Mary kept trust in God,
we pray to the Lord:
ALL: O Key of David, open for us the way to God!

Presider: In hope, let us pray as Jesus taught us:
ALL: Our Father . . .

Presider: In loving trust and faith, O God,
your daughter Mary accepted your will for her
to bring into the world your Son, the Messiah.
May we embrace her spirit of humility,
her faith in your loving providence,
her trust in your covenant with your people,
so that Christ may find a dwelling place in us
and that we may bring his light and peace
into our own time and place.
We ask this in the name of your Son,
Jesus, the long-awaited Messiah.

ALL: Amen.

BLESSING

Presider: May grace and peace be given to us in abundance
as we come to know God in Jesus, the Christ.
To God be glory for ever and ever. *[2 Peter 3:18]*

ALL: Amen.

OR

[Table Blessing:]

Presider: For your many gifts,
we give you thanks, O Lord.
May our home be a place of warmth and love;
may all who come to our table
be welcomed as would Christ.

ALL: Amen.

December 21

THE *LUCERNARIUM*

As three or four candles are lighted:

Acolyte: O radiant Dawn,
Splendor of eternal light,
Sun of justice:

ALL: **Come, light the way of those lost in darkness;
shine on those who dwell in the shadow of death!**

THE WORD OF GOD   *Luke 1:39-45*

Lector: From the Gospel of Luke.

Mary set out and went with haste
to a Judean town in the hill country,
where she entered the house of Zechariah
and greeted Elizabeth.
When Elizabeth heard Mary's greeting,
the child leaped in her womb.
And Elizabeth was filled with the Holy Spirit
and exclaimed with a loud cry,
"Blessed are you among women,
and blessed is the fruit of your womb.
And why has this happened to me,
that the mother of my Lord comes to me?
For as soon as I heard the sound of your greeting,
the child in my womb leaped for joy.
And blessed is she who believed
that there would be a fulfillment
of what was spoken to her by the Lord."

A brief pause follows for silent reflection.

PRAYERS

Presider: As Mary and Elizabeth came together as family,

let us, too, come together as family
to offer prayer and praise to our God:

That we may respond in loving charity
to those in need
as did Mary in her care of Elizabeth,
we pray to the Lord:

ALL: O Sun of justice, illuminate the darkness!

Presider: That parents-to-be may be blessed
with wisdom and love
to carry out the holy vocations of
motherhood and fatherhood,
we pray to the Lord:

ALL: O Sun of justice, illuminate the darkness!

Presider: That we may always place our trust and hope
in the providence of God,
we pray to the Lord:

ALL: O Sun of justice, illuminate the darkness!

Presider: Let us join our hearts and voices as one family
to offer the prayer that Jesus taught us:

ALL: Our Father . . .

Presider: O God, in response to your word to her,
Mary went "in haste" to be with Elizabeth
in her time of need.
May we respond to the good news of Christ's
coming
by imitating her joyful humility,
putting ourselves willingly and happily
at the service of one another.
We ask this in the name of your Son,
Jesus the Christ.

ALL: Amen.

BLESSING

Presider: May the peace of God reign in our hearts.

May God's Word dwell in us always.
In all our words and actions
let us give thanks to our Father
in the name of the Lord Jesus.

[Colossians 3:15, 16, 17]

ALL: Amen.

OR

[Table Blessing:]
Presider: May our joyful sharing
with our brothers and sisters
of every good thing you have given us,
be our song of thanks to you,
God of compassion,
Lord of life and Father of all.

ALL: Amen.

December 22

THE *LUCERNARIUM*

> *As three or four candles are lighted:*

Acolyte: O Ruler of all nations,
O Joy of every heart,
O Keystone of all humanity:

ALL: **Come, save the people you have made your own!**

THE WORD OF GOD *Luke 1:46-55*

Lector: From the Gospel of Luke.

Mary said to Elizabeth,
"My soul magnifies the Lord,
and my spirit rejoices in God my Savior,
for he has looked with favor
on the lowliness of his servant.
Surely, from now on
all generations will call me blessed;
for the Mighty One has done great things for me,
and holy is his name.
His mercy is for those who fear him
from generation to generation.
He has shown strength with his arm;
he has scattered the proud
    in the thoughts of their hearts.
He has brought down the powerful
    from their thrones,
and lifted up the lowly;
he has filled the hungry with good things,
and sent the rich away empty.
He has helped his servant Israel,
in remembrance of his mercy,
according to the promise he made to our
    ancestors,
to Abraham and to his descendants forever."

A brief pause follows for silent reflection.

PRAYERS

Presider: Let us join in Mary's song of praise:

That everything we do may proclaim
the goodness of God,
we pray to the Lord:
ALL: O Joy of every heart, hear us!

Presider: That we may both give and receive
the mercy of God,
we pray to the Lord:
ALL: O Joy of every heart, hear us!

Presider: That we may find our joy and fulfillment
in being servants of God,
we pray to the Lord:
ALL: O Joy of every heart, hear us!

Presider: Jesus revealed to us the wonders of God our
Father;
and so, we pray with joyful confidence:
ALL: Our Father . . .

Presider: Gracious God,
we joyfully await the dawning of your Light,
Jesus Christ.
May the light of his word
shatter the darkness of ignorance and greed;
may the warmth of his love
melt the winter of hatred and injustice.
Transform us into a people of his light,
that we may reflect your saving grace
to our waiting world.
We ask this in the name of your Son,
Jesus, your Light to all nations.
ALL: Amen.

BLESSING

Presider: May God be glorified in all of us through Christ.
To God be glory and honor forever and ever.

[1 Peter 4:11]

ALL: Amen.

OR

[Table Blessing:]
Presider: Father, we eagerly await the coming
of your greatest gift to us, Jesus Christ.
Bless these gifts and bless us,
that we may always live
in the light and peace of Christ,
your Word of light and peace to us.

ALL: Amen.

December 23

THE *LUCERNARIUM*

As three or four candles are lighted:

Acolyte: O Emmanuel,
Desire of the nations,
Savior of all people:

ALL: Come, set us free and save us, Lord our God!

THE WORD OF GOD   *Micah 5:2, 4-5*

Lector: From the prophet Micah.

You, O Bethlehem of Ephrathah,
who are one of the little clans of Judah,
from you shall come forth for me
one who is to rule in Israel,
whose origin is from old,
from ancient days.
He shall stand and feed his flock
in the strength of the Lord,
in the majesty of the name of the Lord his God.
And they will live secure,
for now he shall be great
to the ends of the earth;
and he shall be the one of peace.

A brief pause follows for silent reflection.

PRAYERS

Presider: As we await the miracle of Bethlehem,
let us offer our prayers to the Lord who comes:

For the gift to see the Lord's glory
   in simple things,
we pray to the Lord:
ALL: O Emmanuel, come and fill us with your love!

Presider: For the gift to rejoice in the Lord's presence
in every moment,
we pray to the Lord:
ALL: O Emmanuel, come and fill us with your love!

Presider: For the gift of peace among all peoples,
we pray to the Lord:
ALL: O Emmanuel, come and fill us with your love!

Presider: Let us offer the prayer Jesus taught
his friends and followers:
ALL: Our Father . . .

Presider: Gracious God, make of our homes and hearts
little "Bethlehems" for our time and place.
In quiet, unseen ways,
may we bring to our broken world
the healing and peace of Jesus the Messiah,
in whose name we offer our prayer.
ALL: Amen.

BLESSING

Presider: May the peace of God
which is beyond all understanding
keep our hearts and minds
in the knowledge and love of God
and of the Father's Son, our Lord Jesus Christ.
[Philippians 4:7]
ALL: Amen.

OR

[Table Blessing:]
Presider: Bless the gifts of this table, O Lord.
May our Advent preparations for your coming
make us worthy one day to enter your presence
and celebrate forever at your table in heaven.
ALL: Amen.

Christmas Eve

THE *LUCERNARIUM*

> *As all four candles are lighted:*

Acolyte: Today you will know that the Lord is coming;

ALL: **and in the morning we will behold God's glory.**

THE WORD OF GOD   *1 John 4:9-11*

Lector: From the first letter of John.

> God's love was revealed among us in this way:
> God sent his only Son into the world
> so that we might live through him.
> In this is love,
> not that we loved God
> but that he loved us
> and sent his Son
> to be the atoning sacrifice for our sins.
> Beloved, since God loved us so much,
> we also ought to love one another.
>
> *[In the evening, one of the two readings for
> Christmas Day—Isaiah 9:2, 5-6 or Luke 2:1-20—
> may be read.]*
>
> *A brief pause follows for silent reflection.*

PRAYERS

Presider: The day of the Lord is near;
in joyful hope, let us offer to God our prayers:

> That we may be blessed with the spirit of
>   simplicity
> that marked Jesus' birth,
> we pray to the Lord:

ALL: **May your birth bring peace to all, O Lord.**

Presider: That we may be blessed with the spirit of joy
that marked Jesus' teachings,
we pray to the Lord:

ALL: May your birth bring peace to all, O Lord.

Presider: That we may be blessed with the spirit of
compassion
that marked Jesus' healing of the sick and
the dying,
we pray to the Lord:

ALL: May your birth bring peace to all, O Lord.

Presider: The Messiah revealed to us
the love of God our Father;
and so, let us pray as one family:

ALL: Our Father . . .

Presider: The long night is over;
we await the dawning of your great light, O God.
May the rising of Christ the Morningstar
fill our home and hearts
with the radiance of your love
every day of every season.
We ask this in the name of your Son,
Jesus, your Radiant Light.

ALL: Amen.

BLESSING

Presider: The grace of God has appeared,
with salvation for all!
May God bless us with kindness and love
this day/night and always!   *[Titus 2:11; 3:4]*

ALL: Amen.

OR

[Table Blessing:]

Presider: Father, we thank you
for bringing us together this day/night
to celebrate the birth of your Son.

May we bring the joy and peace of this day/night to every place, in every season.

ALL: Amen.

Christmas Day

THE *LUCERNARIUM*

As four white candles are lighted:

Acolyte: Let the heavens be glad and the earth exult:

ALL: For Christ the Savior is born for us! Alleluia!

THE WORD OF GOD

Lector: From the prophet Isaiah.   *Isaiah 9:2, 6-7*

The people who walked in darkness
have seen a great light;
those who lived in a land of deep darkness—
on them light has shined.
For a child has been born for us,
a son given to us;
authority rests upon his shoulders;
and he is named Wonderful Counselor, Mighty God,
Everlasting Father, Prince of Peace.
His authority shall grow continually,
and there shall be endless peace
for the throne of David and his kingdom.
He will establish and uphold it
with justice and with righteousness
from this time onward and forevermore.
The zeal of the Lord of hosts will do this.

OR

Lector: From the Gospel of Luke.   *Luke 2:1-20*

In those days
    a decree went out from Emperor Augustus
that all the world should be registered.
This was the first registration
and was taken while Quirinius was governor of
    Syria.

All went out to their own towns to be registered.
Joseph also went from the town of Nazareth in
    Galilee
to Judea, to the city of David called Bethlehem,
because he was descended from the house and
    family of David.
He went to be registered with Mary,
to whom he was engaged
    and who was expecting a child.
While they were there,
the time came for her to deliver her child.
And she gave birth to her firstborn son
and wrapped him in bands of cloth,
and laid him in a manger,
because there was no place for them in the inn.

In the region
there were shepherds living in the fields,
keeping watch over their flock by night.
Then an angel of the Lord stood before them,
and the glory of the Lord shone around them,
and they were terrified.
But the angel said to them,
"Do not be afraid; for see—
I am bringing you good news of great joy
    for all people:
to you is born this day in the city of David
a Savior, who is the Messiah, the Lord.
This will be a sign for you:
you will find a child wrapped in bands of cloth
and lying in a manger."
And suddenly there was with the angel
a multitude of the heavenly host,
praising God and saying,
"Glory to God in the highest heaven,
and on earth peace among those whom he favors."

When the angels had left them and gone into
    heaven,
the shepherds said to one another,
"Let us go now to Bethlehem

and see this thing that has taken place,
which the Lord has made known to us."
So they went in haste
and found Mary and Joseph,
and the child lying in a manger.
When they saw this,
they made known what had been told them
   about this child;
and all who heard it were amazed
at what the shepherds told them.
But Mary treasured all these things
and pondered them in her heart.
The shepherds returned,
glorifying and praising God
for all they had heard and seen,
as it had been told them.

A brief pause follows for silent reflection.

PRAYERS

Presider: Today, heaven and earth are one.
God our Savior is in our midst.
Let us join our hearts in prayer:

That today may not be the end
of our Christmas celebration,
but an everlasting season of peace,
we pray to the Lord:
ALL: Let the earth ring out for joy, for you have come!

Presider: That compassion, forgiveness, joy and hope
may be the true gifts we give and receive this day,
we pray to the Lord:
ALL: Let the earth ring out for joy, for you have come!

Presider: That God will bless
our loved ones who could not be here,
our relatives and friends who are with God,
the poor, the sick and the dying,
and all who must spend this day alone,

we pray to the Lord:
ALL: Let the earth ring out for joy, for you have come!

Presider: Let us now pray together the words
that Jesus taught us during his life among us:
ALL: Our Father . . .

Presider: Child of Bethlehem, house of bread;
Man of Jerusalem, city of peace;
you have loved us without limit or condition,
in our greatness and in our misery,
in our folly and in our virtue;
may your hand be always upon us
and may your heart be within us
so that we, too,
may become bread and peace
for one another.*
ALL: Amen.

BLESSING

Presider: The grace of God has appeared,
with salvation for all!
May God bless us with kindness and love
this day and always!   *[Titus 2:11; 3:4]*
ALL: Amen.

OR

[Table Blessing:]
Presider: Gracious God,
bless our celebration of your Son's birth.
May our hearts welcome him
and his Gospel of peace
to all people of good will.
ALL: Amen.

*Prayer composed by John Hammond, O.S.B. Copyright 1975 by
The Benedictine Foundation of the State of Vermont, Inc. Weston
Priory, Weston, Vermont. Reprinted with permission.